Mastery of public speaking.

It's work, and refining a skill.

Not a wish or a dream or a goal.

A skill.

Commit to the time it takes to master it.

Get the feedback you need.

Use this book as a tool to help you - but nothing replaces going out and standing up and giving your talk then learning from the "Live" experience.

Congratulations on taking this step.

Mark Davis

www.MasterTheArtOfPublicSpeaking.com

***

FREE BOOK OFFER -
"You Don't Get Any Better at Public Speaking
Sitting in Your Chair!"

Quotations for public speakers and those wanting to be more confident

***

Be the first to get the next book in the "Master The Art" series **FREE**! Subscribers only.
Books scheduled for release in 2015 include:

Master The Art of Training
Master The Art of Sales Presentations
Master The Art of Online Communication

Just visit the website and subscribe to the Free Book updates and "Master The Art" Speaking tips and strategies.

Get regular tips, advance notice of new books and their free promotion periods, as well as the chance to provide stories for future books!

As always, feel free to leave a review where you bought this book. They are always appreciated. Your stories are always welcomed and might even be included in a future volume!

For speaking inquiries or workshops around the world, send an email to Mark@MasterTheArtOfPublicSpeaking.com or find the author on Facebook or Linked In as Coach Mark Davis.

www.MasterTheArtOfPublicSpeaking.com

CHAPTER ONE
The Power Of The Stage

In the audience with 8000 other people I'm standing, singing, waving my arms, and loving every minute of it.

U2 are playing in Melbourne, with BB King and his band accompanying, on the "When Love Comes To Town" tour of 1989. I'd only started listening to U2 the year before, when a bohemian student at University played CD's at a camp. All night. I loved it, the rock and roll, the passion, the sense of purpose behind the lyrics. At the time I was still getting used to University life, living just off the campus, but meeting new friends, discovering new things.

This was music I could get right into, and when the concert came around, I had to go! I'd been playing Rattle & Hum Live on cassette for about 6 months, and it was wearing out! But I knew the words to the songs, and the group of us that went said it was a great concert and we were full of adrenalin all the way home.

The live performance was something surreal, after only hearing the music in the one dimension, on headphones, in the car, in my room. This was a 3-D experience with music so loud I felt I would never hear anything else again.

The lights, the stage, the 'presence' of Bono and the confidence with which he owned the stage and performed to every person there.

He performed for me.

The feeling that this song was being played — not for 8000 people — but for me! I knew these songs, I closed my eyes and we sang it together.

When BB King started playing his riffs for "When Love Comes To Town", I was doing the air guitar up in my seat. Because I had already lived the song. Had already felt the feelings and belted out the words so many times. Now it was all coming together. For me.

The point I want you to understand, is that this entire concert, every monologue, every syllable, every note. Was for me. One person.

And the best bands in the world understand that if you can connect with just one person - you've got everyone! Because only one person is listening to this song right now.

When you speak on stage, only one person is listening. So you have to speak as if there is only one person.

No-one is listening on other peoples behalf. No-one is receiving the information as part of a massive mind-collective.

Each individual hears it for themselves.

And thats why audience for great speakers say things like -
"She spoke to me."
"I could really relate."
"He made it easy for me to grasp the key concepts"
"It was the right time for me to hear what she was saying."
A good speaker has multiple layers of their talk. So that people at all levels can take it in, and act upon it. Its pitched for the beginner and the expert. The one that knows nothing, and the one who "knows it all".

So everyone can get what they need from the talk.

Humour is great for some people, but not all. As a tool its useful for everyone because it releases pressure and can help people take the talk less seriously, or to not think so hard.

Being intelligent on stage might be good for other academics, but not necessarily for people with lower IQ, or less book-smarts.

If you are only speaking to one person, like I am writing this book, speaking to you (not your neighbour who is mowing the lawn at the ungodly hour of 730am) then you have to assume that one person is an 'everyman'.

What I mean by that is you want to write your speech/talk and delivery it as if there is only one person in the entire room, that has all the qualities of all the people you want to get your message through to.

This is hard.

But, the first question I recommend asking yourself when you want to speak on any stage is this.

"How much are you willing to risk?"

The higher the level of preparation you put in, means you're going to have more invested in getting your message across. And you'll be less inclined to be lazy.

It's not just about getting up there and telling people what you know, just as acting isn't about getting in front of an audience and hoping that they like the way that you do your hair.

The audience will tell you very, very quickly if you're connecting, and you do that by being willing to risk something. Risking that people may not like you.

Beyond that there is another deeper layer of insecurity that you need to get past.

It's the risk of looking vulnerable. If you are vulnerable, you can be hurt. But if you have added a layer of detachment and separated yourself personally from your message, you can let your talk do the 'talking'.

Vulnerability takes us a layer below the surface, into what makes you tick. Into the why you do it.

People respect that and becuase they don't listen as a group, they are going to feel things about you as an individual.

Imagine this.

You walk out onto the stage, reach your hand deep into your chest, pluck out your heart and hold it up, pumping and glistening.

Take a deep breath and... You share with your audience what is true for you. Your message that you have worked so hard to prepare and deliver for that one person in the audience.

It's what you're passionate about, why you care.

And they believe you. Because they can tell you have a reason for what you are doing, it is a part of you, that you have now shared with them. Beliefs are the hardest things to change in people. Beliefs lead to the habits we have each day and the actions that those around us see. So to change someone else's.... Very difficult.

Sharing our own beliefs, thats just as hard, because of the vulnerability behind it. But when we have the confidence, sharing those beliefs as a matter of fact, not trying to change someone else — thats powerful.

It gives us respect and they trust us more because of that opening up and sharing that we do. If someone believes you, your words, your music, your movie performance - its because we see the depth of that belief and conviction. You consciously make the decision to suspend reality in movies to believe that Will Smith is Mohammed Ali, that Michael Douglas is Liberace, that Cate Blanchett is Queen Elizabeth.

Because you want to believe.
We all want to believe.

Your audience will connect with you because a good speaker creates moments that can be shared. Moments that have the potential to create a bond. Quotations that you will remember and tell others about. Emotions (usually in a story) or lesson that you have learned. What you gained from an experience - they can to. The mistakes you made that you own up to, that you have no pride about sharing. The lack of keeping secret these powerful lessons helps open a door for your audience to share themselves, knowing that its ok to do so.

They empathise, because a good speaker shares stories from their life that everyone can relate to. These are called "Universal" stories, and range from talking about a dysfunctional family, to divorce, to feeling displaced, not knowing your place in the world, to friendships, to money, and the list goes on.

Empathy is always more powerful no just when they put themselves in your shoes, but when they have BEEN in the same shoes. And a good speaker knows how to do that. Or a songwriter, who bonds to people around the world who have experienced the same thing.

Never forget the power of Country Music.

Its tales of love and loss, of heartbreak and of devastation. And of the redeeming power of love and forgiveness and getting back on your feet to try again. Everyone can relate.

They listen. Because nothing is as compelling as a personal story that opens a wound, reveals a flaw, peels back the layers, and shows the vulnerability of the speaker.

And you can hold an audiences attention for a long time when you do this. In the training edition of this series you can learn more about how to apply this for teaching, for now just focus on the power of getting up close and personal.

They laugh. Sometimes they laugh because what you say, is funny. Often its the bittersweet laugh of empathy, or the nervous laugh of someone who doesn't want admit the truth as the story or talk applies to them. But that release, that emotional response, is proof enough that a speaker is doing their job.

They cry. Some of them do. With happiness or with sadness. You don't want to be known as the speaker that makes everyone cry, but you do want people to retell your stories and the emotions they created for your audience. That will build your audience and get you repeat business as past attendees bring their friends and colleagues.

They applaud.

Because they respect you and what you've one.

How you have changed their life even a little in that time you were performing.

Just like I applauded every song that was sung at that concert.

Picture this alternative.

You walk out on stage with your clothes tightly wrapped around you.

You stand behind a 4-foot podium. You read your notes.

You show a PowerPoint presentation. You avoid eye contact.

Your audience is separate, distinct and apart from you.

No connection, no heart, no soul, no spirit.

No empathy, no sense of unity.

No cheers, no tears, no hugs of joy afterward.

No applause with any heart or soul in it

What's the point?

People want to speak because they will experience the power of the stage. The amazing, thrilling, adrenaline-packed experience of offering people a transformational experience.

I bought the t-shirt at the concert and wore it for a year.

If you walk out of a talk and then 5 minutes later go, "what did I get from that" then the speaker failed.

If you don't come out buzzing, with pages of notes, and controversial topics over coffee tomorrow or a quote you can't help repeating, or a song you keep singing, a label or a topic that just has you hooked - the speaker failed.

Here's another tip that will help you know how you're going. I know that its hard to stop midway through your talk and take a quick survey of how people are liking it. That's what your feedback partner is for, to give you what you need in that area. See book one for details or the website for the downloadable feedback form.

The audience is really just one great big mirror.

Whatever you are sending 'out' to your audience, will come back.

So if you think it's a bad audience, it's a result of your projection. If you see sad faces, people falling asleep, or ones that are even looking angry... Its all your responsibility.

You can't blame the previous speaker, the weather, the economy. It's you.

Turning that around comes with experience and relies on you to be able to change up your style, something we're going to work on in a later chapter. Your style may be boring. That will definitely show up in the faces and body posture of your audience.

Lying back, looking disinterested? Time to up your speed and volume and variety.

All looking angry? Change topic from something so negative or attacking, and shift to a lighter topic.

If they are all leaning forward, taking notes, nodding, laughing on cue, and the room is warming up and you feel like you are full of energy - something's probably going right.

If you feel from the audience a connection, a willingness to explore with you, to trust you and listen, experience vicariously an adventure with you... you've got more of the power of the stage. And that should inspire you to keep working hard and spend the time you need to get the outcome again and again. And give that audience even more value.

And in the tradition of music and movies, from Spiderman 2 (Tobey Maguire version) - "With great power comes great responsibility". Use your power to influence and inspire well, and go help change people's lives.

Let's go find out how we master this skill, shall we? Because it's all about caring, and not caring.

CHAPTER TWO
Mastery is caring... and not caring

What's the big secret to public speaking?

Surely it's not that complicated.

Let me tell you a quick story about a friend of mine, Jerry Clark. Jerry does over 100 live performances a year in dozens of countries around the world.

We were driving in New Zealand a few years back, when I asked him about getting sick when speaking. And if he wasn't quite 100% health wise, did he ever cancel.

He told me something he heard early in his speaking career.

The speaker who shared this had been in the game for over 30 years, as a philosopher. A mentor respected and revered by every student of personal development.

He told Jerry, that the secret to performing well was not about how you were feeling. An audience just wants what you have stood up to share.

So he gave this piece of advice for when you don't feel well, or don't WANT to get up and talk. When you think that the audience could be negative, or if you are seeking approval.

"Hide your need and show your skill"

It's my belief that people want you to inspire them.

They would not be in your audience unless a part of them wanted what you have to say whether they know it or not.

It's your responsibility to give it everything you've got.

Every time.

And when you make the commitment to go up on the stage and speak, miracles happen.

It's not magic, but some guiding force looks after you, and helps you to deliver your message. When it's your message, and your audience that you focus on. Not the other way around.

Hide your need.

If you're sick, they aren't interested. But they will admire you more for speaking through it if they ever find out. Continue your talk, and take time everyday to work on your health for the future so you're ready to deliver your message.

If you want approval for your ability to teach or train, STOP! They aren't interested. And you don't need their approval.

If you want them to be positive because you think they are negative - they will see your nerves and negativity reflected back on them. Focus on your message.

Show your skill.

Its not memorising words.

Or getting rid of your fears.

Its definitely not the way you look or how intelligent you sound.

And it's not visualising people naked.

You have to care about getting your message out there.

And then, at the same time, you have to stop caring about what people think about you. This helps you to spend the time practicing and get better at your craft.

Mastery is about getting your 'EGO' out of the way, to focus on your message.

Remember! The audience couldn't care less about you.

All they care about is what they can learn from you.

The value you offer them that they can take with them when your talk is over.

The memorable quotes, those audio gems. And the strategies, the ideas, the motivation, the inspiration you gave.

You are just the channel that the information comes through. The path to help them get where they want faster.

Now I could ask you to not take it personally, even though you will.

I know that as you read this, you're thinking all sorts of defensive statements, like ...

"Who does he think he is? I'm a great speaker, and my audiences love me";

"What do you mean? Does that make all my preparation time a waste? Preparing my look, my words, my slides. All the coaching and acting practice, my years of experience, my knowledge."

"You must be a bad speaker, because you haven't experienced the responses from a crowd I have."

I am not here to argue with you in this book, instead to share my opinion on what makes a great speaker. And I know you want to be great.

The more you care about your audience, and focus on getting the delivery of what you have to say right, the easier it is for them to respect you.

"Don't let the messenger, get in the way of the message!"

That means getting yourself out of the way of your message.

It's the only way that you can share information, your message, and have it accepted by your audience.

People do learn to love certain speakers and it's wonderful to be in an audience when people do like you.

Focus on giving the best possible presentation first, and the rest will take care of itself.

They are there for them. Not you.

Stop taking yourself so seriously, and get down to the business of delivering the best possible message. That's why we speak.

If you have an audience sitting in their chairs ready to listen to you... START!

And make it worth their while.

Give them everything

I once discussed the topic of sharing 'teaser' information with a client.

"Why?" He asked. "To get the best out of your audience's responses, Give them everything!"

When you impress them with your knowledge today, you will have more to share the next time. And that is because you were willing to hold nothing back, and next time you know more!

We cannot expect people to keep 100% of what we tell them, in fact we're lucky if they remember 10-20%!

It's just our nature, to remember what interests us and what is relevant to them right at that moment.

This is why you can deliver the same talk word for word, to the same audience a week or a month later. They will find different parts that interest them. Even a year later - or 10 years later!

My good friend Gail was in my Houston workshop recently. He attended 12 years ago, and it was almost exactly the same workshop! But because he had changed over time, and I had changed too, he still got value from being there. The same message, heard at two moments in time, can be a unique experience. We hear what we need to, when the time is right.

Inspiration

The chance to inspire someone to change, to take a look inside themselves, to use the knowledge that you've built up. That's a great reason to speak.

You'll make a difference for at least one person in every audience. For most speakers, that's the motivating force to get up and speak. No one wants the audience to ignore or forget them, but at the same time you can't expect everyone to think you're the greatest ever. Keep focusing on that one person. Because you don't know which one it is! That keeps you committed to inspiring every individual in your audience.

This chapter is the only one you need

1. If you prepared well, you won't be focusing on yourself. Then you won't be worrying about the audience's response. You'll be 100% involved in your material and delivering it for maximum impact. Prepare, prepare, prepare. Professionals get paid to present what they've prepared and practiced. My first book on this topic taught this, so if you haven't read it yet, I recommend you get it on Amazon today and read it alongside this one.

2. Every time I go on stage in front of an audience I'm committed to making a difference. I align with my vision for that talk. And because I know the information is good, I do everything to focus on the people and give the best talk I can. No excuses.

3. And don't waste people's time by forgetting those two things. If you read my first book you will know every idea works. Don't get lazy or think you can take the shortcuts. Speaking is a profession and those who do it well get paid well. Keep the standard up!

Mastery of this skill comes with time. So it's now time to get started by understanding the simplest tip to getting your audience to like you.

CHAPTER THREE
Where are you?

Lights go down, audience applause finishes as you walk up onto the stage.

"Good Evening Cleveland, great to be back!"

Deathly silence.

Because you're in Pittsburgh.

First thing every speaker needs to remember, especially if they are moving around and presenting in a variety of areas.

Remember where you are! And tell your audience you know where you are!

Its one of the most personal things you can do to build a connection with your audience.

Everyone in the audience lives where you're speaking. They work there. They may have gone to school there. Their kids live there. Their parents.

You have to know where you are, and acknowledge it.

At the beginning. Not in the middle, not at the end, but right up front.

This will give you an advantage over your audience as you already 'know them' more than they know you. It will encourage them to lean forward and listen because you are already 'local'. It builds rapport and it builds trust.

I have a few simple tips for you to make this work to your advantage.

Be Here Now.

Where you were - they don't want to know. Where you're going - they don't want to know.

Never mention where you were yesterday. Because no-one cares. They don't. And because people will always compare in their own mind they will feel you mentioning another town or city means you like it more. Or you wish you were there. Or the people there are smarter, more good looking.

I know it doesn't make sense to you. But people are insecure, especially when they are nervous about listening to someone they don't know.

If you talk about where you're going - thats just as bad! It makes your audience think that you don't want to be there and can't wait to leave. That the future is more exciting than the present. If you live in the present, as you should, then focusing on the people in front of you will give the best possible reaction.

Staying positive

People will always defend if you attack. So it's a good idea to never say negative things about where you are, or where you were.

Imagine if you heard a speaker say, "It's great to be here in West LA. I was in East LA yesterday and I'm glad to be away from there!" What if half the audience lives in East LA and came here because it's where the talk is? You just alienated half your audience.

Or "Thank goodness I've left Chicago, their weather is so windy and my hair got blown every which way!" Won't help if you're at a national conference where 30% of the audience is from Chicago. Also bad form if it just started raining outside. Then someone pulls out their phone saying how beautiful weather in Chicago is right now.

If you talk at one school don't talk about another school and how many of their students finish in the top % at the end of high school.

If you are a guest at a church - don't talk about how big another church is or how motivational their pastor is.

Speaking to a hotel chain? Remember the name and remember the location. Don't refer to competitors comfortable beds and giant bathtubs.

If you walk into a Fortune 500 company or ASX200 office, don't comment on the chairs. Be careful not to compare the paintings, the carpet or the suits.

It is one of the greatest sins

And if your audience forgives you, they have still discounted your value as an amateur, not a professional. And that means less impact from your talk, and less repeat business.

That means its important to focus on knowing where you are in your preparation for this talk.

So lets look at the preparation you can do.

For the city you are visiting:

Read a copy of the local paper online a day to a week before. See what the main issues are in the town.

Find out the name of the Mayor. There are people in your audience who will have an opinion and engage with you when you mention their name. But remember you are mentioning it to show you know where you are, not passing judgement or starting a topic that could go on forever. Keep in control.

Know the history of the town or city where you are talking. Who built it or settled there. The origin of the name, which may be indigenous or named after a famous person.

For bonus points in this area, get a local person to introduce you. You will talk to them beforehand, and learn their name, their family situation. If you have more time, discover their goals, their job, and say nice things about them on the stage when you start.

Drink the water. Never appear afraid to drink the water unless a local tells you not to. And don't comment on it as it will always come across as criticism. For example, Brisbane water tasted like a swimming pool 10 years ago, and in some hotels its still the same. But locals are used to it.

Don't put your foot in it and offend them.

Try the local food speciality - if you're in New England, try Clam Chowder, if you're in Naples, eat some pizza. In Texas? Get some Tex-Mex, and if you're in Thailand, eat a Pad Thai noodle dish. Loving local food is like loving the locals. Then reference it in your talk.

Know the weather pattern of the area, so you can comment on the snow being normal or unseasonable. If you say its hot in Phoenix Arizona in winter, they will laugh at you. That may work too! But you can't get angry at the weather, because they live there and deal with it every day. I lived in Melbourne for over 20 years, and we have four seasons in one day. So we aren't upset by it. But if a visitor came to town and complained, we disregard them as rude.

For a company where you are speaking:

Know the company vision, mission, goals, purpose.

Know the name of the CEO.

Know who invited you, who is introducing you, and who is paying you!

What's the product range?

Where does the company have offices? Just this one, or all over the place? Which one is the most successful?

Is the company growing?

How new is it - does it fit the category of startup? Are they traditional with Directors and investors, or did they use crowdfunding or Philanthropy? If they are Non-Profit, are they a Charity? Only 1 in 10 Non-Profits fit that category in Australia, and it makes a big difference to how they operate.

You can find all this out in a simple email to the person who organised you to speak.

Then you need to work it into your presentation opening, as you say your "Thank You" to the relevant parties. Then people feel acknowledged and valued and they lean forward and like you more.

If the business is in a competitive sector like a Hotel/Hospitality

How old is the building?
When did the hotel open?
Who is the manager?
How is the business doing? Just an opinion is enough.
How many staff?
Who is the main competitor?
What makes them different?
Are they admired or hated? Finding out the attitude means you can align rather than create a point of argument. If they respect the competitor, you don't want to say "Let's Crush the Opposition!"

If the business is a startup they are usually growing and making a name for themselves.
But you need to know so that you can tailor your business to growth and positivity. A message for a 50 year old business is different to that for a startup.

Speaking at a school?

Who's the principal?
How old is the school?
How many students?
How many teachers?

Do they get a lot of funding, as a disadvantaged school?

Or are they a private school with high fees?

Is the area the school is in high, middle, low class?

What year level are you speaking to, and how many kids? 10 is different to 100. You need different strategies.

Is there a uniform?

Is the school strict?

Who is the favourite teacher?

Who is the weirdest/strangest teacher?

How successful is the school at getting kids into University?

How successful is the school at sport?

What else makes them unique?

What other challenges do they have?

Speaking at a church?

Who is the pastor/minister/priest?

How many people attend/will be in the audience?

Whats the demographics?

How wealthy are the attendees?

What is the ethnic mix?

Who is the most influential congregation menber?

What is their policy on sales of items you as a speaker might sell?

How should you present to get a repeat invitation?

When was the building constructed?

How was that funded?

What are the churches goals for growth/relevance/staying alive?

These basic questions will give you a base to frame and shape the first impression you give when you start talking.

They help make the audience feel at ease that you "know them".

No-one listens to strangers, but we do listen to friends, and people that "understand" us.

It's possible for us to listen to a total stranger because this principle is so powerful. It works. It's also possible for us to structure our talk to be that stranger who is an instantly respected source of information.

After thousands of talks around the world, I can tell you this works.

I have never met a stranger, even though I have talked to thousands of people around the world. Once I meet a new person and have a conversation 1:1 or them in my audience of 1000, we have a connection. It's like we have known each other forever. After my presentations, they feel they know me.

I want you to understand - this is by design. Not luck.

The better understand your audience, the more a part of their life you are for that moment in time. The more they know you, the more they trust you. And when they trust you, you have a better chance they will act on what you say, and the more they want to hear more from you.

The opposite is also true.

I want you to think for a moment about a situation like this:

Speaker comes to town, gives a talk. Mentions how beautiful the beaches were last week when they were on vacation. Says they don't remember the last time they were in your town. But they just can't wait to see the big parade on Sunday in the next place they are going to.

Asks how to pronounce the name of your town but still gets it wrong. Doesn't mention the organiser, the sponsor, or thank anyone.

It doesn't matter how valuable your presentation is if you don't build rapport with your audience. It's going to be an uphill battle trying to get your message across.

And they will forget you just as quick, except when someone mentions your name and brings up how bad you were.

One of the challenges in this area of course is when you change locations for 3 or 4 meetings or presentations per day. Or you change cities every other day.

But the time you invest in knowing where you are is worth it, I guarantee it.

Repeat business becomes easy as they will ask you to speak again. You will grow a customer and referral base that will share with other audiences encouraging you to have you speak to them. And that makes you more money or gives you more audiences to share your message with.

I did many in-home trainings on public speaking in my socks, comfortable clothes and with the aroma from the dinner still in the air. Invited to speak and share what I knew with intimate audiences.

The reason home presentations work is because people are comfortable in their home. Insurance, Network Marketing, Bankers, Electricity and other industries love the home presentation so much. You have people where they are familiar , and if you can be comfortable in their home, then they adopt you into their family. Respect the family, become a 'local' and your presentation becomes easy.

Knowing enough about "Where you Are" is important. And it's why you have to focus on the audience and their surroundings even more than you focus on yourself. When you do that, they feel like you care. And they they will listen.

So now you know where you are, let's look at how people take information in, so you can get as much of yours accepted by your audience.

CHAPTER FOUR
How do you read?

How I taught 5 year old's to read and enjoy it!

Reading is a key to better speaking. We create our research material, and we grow our knowledge base, we discover new words and new ways of describing things. We go inside someone else's head.

When we read, we are also accessing the part of the brain that our audience is using when they listen to us. It is where we read to ourselves out loud in our response to what we are hearing or seeing - or doing!

If we can learn right now, how people take information in, we will be able to prepare better talks.

Sitting quietly in the classroom staring hard at the pages of a book that just didn't quite make sense, Tim was having a tough time.

It wasn't just the words, which for a 5 year old appeared to be endless jumbles of vowels and consonants. There was no obvious order and they didn't make any sense.

The 9 attempts Tim had made to pronounce this one tricky word all fell flat. The gentle encouragement from the assistant teacher not helping. His rapidly deflating balloon of self-esteem was devasting to watch.

Each guess at these impossible words was less energetic, less passionate and fatalistic.

He seemed to be thinking, "what's the point".

Giving up was written all over his face.

Instead of trying harder, it became obvious that he had a strategy. By getting a wrong answer enough times, the answer would finally be given to you. If you just stopped trying, the help would arrive. Seeing him give up, I knew that there had to be a better way to reach the goal, that of a fluent, confident reader.

As a parent helper with the reading programme at the local school every Wednesday I would visit and help. That meant working with the kids and getting them excited about reading. Every parent helped develop the skills to confidently read, comprehend and write.

Like in the movies where they say "no-one gets left behind", it's just like that in the modern 1st grade classroom. Parents assist teachers, so that no kid gets left behind.

But I'm not one to follow all the classroom rules, due to my impatience at the pace of most teaching which follows a strict curriculum.

So I started working with Tim and other students to make their experience of reading and writing more enjoyable.

You see I've found that learning is just not fun - most of the time.

Most learning is a challenge to beat the bell curve, to fight those who naturally find learning easy. Some kids have a headstart because they're older. Others just seem to love studying and learning.

I know I was. Kids and even the teachers occasionally resented it. I was smart enough to be brought forward one grade.

The "brainy chatterbox" from grade 4 now was sitting with the older kids, because he's so smart. Of course it didn't help that I agreed with this.

Anyway, the problem with sticking out from a crowd in either direction, is that you get attention. Good, bad, I don't think that's the point. The point is you are singled out.

I think those kids who are smarter academically get it easier at school, because they can coast a bit. Not have the pressure to work, just enjoy the social aspects.

Anyway back to Tim.

The following weeks, when I sat down with these kids for reading, I took a whole new, radical approach.

Note: This is not being taught in schools.

I sat down with Tim, asked him how he'd gone with the book he had borrowed the day before, and he said it was OK.

The I asked him a crazy question.

"Do you think you could read it to me upside-down?"

Well the look on his face turned from horror of the task ahead to "What?"

Which was exactly what I wanted.

I asked him to read it upside down. Just to try it, see how he went.

And if it didn't work, we'd turn it back the other way.

We were sitting on the chairs in the traditional way, so I said to him, "Do you want to lie on the ground and read? It might be more comfortable."

He said OK, so we lay on the floor, looking at the ceiling of the classroom, holding the book upside-down.

He glanced across at me, now totally sure that I was crazy.

I said, "let's begin".

And he read the entire book upside down.

Now, it was just 5 or 6 words per page, and he could have read it right-side up. But that was hard work.

Suddenly, we'd turned hard work into something that was an adventure, and ridiculous.

His attitude changed, his demeanour shifted from quiet and shy and worried about reading. Now he was laughing and kicking his legs around and tapping them on the ground as he read this book which I held upside down.

Of course, word got around.

Other kids would show up to read over the coming weeks, and they, too, wanted to read upside-down.

I challenged them. "You can't read it upside-down!" They did it anyway, just to prove to me that they could.

(It's usually the fastest way to get a kid to do anything, tell them they can't. You just have to be clever how you use it!)

They showed up, some of them, and opened the book upside- down and just began reading. Laughing, grinning at my looks of amazement as they succeeded at this "impossible" task.

I had they shyest, quietest kids coming up to me and hugging me.

Some of them wouldn't read with me **unless** they could turn it upside-down.

Sometimes I made them read with their eyes shut. That was a challenge. But when there was a pattern, a sequence, any sort of repetition in the book, they'd already memorized it.

And so I got them reading. And loving it!

I do remember a parent or two coming up to me and saying, "Robert loves to read to me upside-down at home. He laughs and laughs while he does that. He says that's what Ben's dad does. Thanks, he's really enjoying his reading. It's not a chore anymore."

I'm not a teacher. I'm a trainer.

I like to think that when I'm working with adults, that I have a good time. My audience learns new things, they like me and they are confident to try and master skills.

All I did was transfer the skills I use when teaching adults, to teaching kids.

I can finally be free to try anything knowing that if I sit back and relax about a problem I can find the answer. I might have to look outside-the box at the problem or situation, but there is a solution!

In my public speaking workshops, I take the shyest people, and teach them confidence in themselves. I don't base this on IQ, or material success or achievement, but by looking inside them and having them be proud of who they are.

Here is my summary of why people work best with supportive, fun, irrational teaching that still gets the job done.

They feel they have permission to learn the way they do it best.

When there is an example being set, it's easier to follow the leader than sticking your own hand on the mousetrap and get it whacked. But if you have permission to make your own mousetrap then you can create a way of learning that never punishes you. It only rewards you for trying.

Just recently, I saw some adults in a training session, and they were struggling. They were just doing the best they can, with the skills they'd developed. Their literacy levels had slipped after 20 years out of school. And the language of the training material was unfamiliar and difficult to understand.

It was all serious, and it appeared that they weren't enjoying the trainig at all, because all they seemed to do was make mistakes.

And without the trainer who can help provide the tools to help them learn better they'll keep going till they get lucky, or just give up.

I hate making mistakes when there's no benefit - even today, especially if I feel like I'm being set up to fail.

So how can you be better as a speaker for your audience, knowing that many of them will find it hard to listen to you?

Keep it Simple.

There is plenty of research to say that most people read at a 7th grade level after they have left school for a few years. I'm not talking about University professors but the average person in your audience.

So if they read at such a low level, you have to be sure you deliver your talk without too much of the following:

- Jargon - that only people in your industry understand. Simplify to the lowest common denominator and more people will nod. That means they get it.
- Big long words with lots of syllables. They sound clever but no-one knows what they mean. Always replace one big word with a few small ones to ensure everyone comprehends your talk.
- Speed - you have to ensure you are talking slow enough that you don't stress people out that they might be missing something. But you have to be speaking fast enough to not put them to sleep!

- Use visual language. Some people like to see stories by making movies in their minds. In fact the more visual you are in teaching, the faster people see themselves in your stories. When you give an example they see themselves doing what you're talking about.
- Have variation in your pitch and volume. Melodic tunes alway sell more than something with only one note. Also the variety keeps the audience listening as the variety is interesting.
- Put feelings into your talk. Some people love to take on the emotions and feelings you put into your talk, and experience it through that sense. These people will hug you after a talk.
- Have some specific statistics or numbers in your talk. This will keep the attention of those fact-obsessed people who love their figures.

Once you have taken enough time to customise your talk, the results will be great. More positive feedback, more engagement, more rapport. That means you got your message across.

Now let's look a little bit more about how understanding why one popular book style teaches us the key to getting our audience to be more interactive with us when we speak.

CHAPTER FIVE
Getting the audience involved

Many speeches get written then read out loud word for word. Politicians read something prepared for them days or weeks in advance. TV news anchors read a teleprompter so they can't make mistakes - every word has been approved by management so it won't offend.

Adults realise that reading is going to be a part of their learning. Textbooks, Training workbooks, DVD instruction manuals are all there to read.

They don't always enjoy it, and there's a reason why. Kids don't like reading as a rule, unless you find a great way to get the information to them so they interact with it and get involved in the book.

Getting kids to read can be difficult. In the 1970's a range of books came out that revolutionised the young reader market and went somewhere that no-one had before.

The concept

The goal with reading is to get people to finish your book. Simple enough concept. That's why as writers we work so hard to make our books interesting.

But with kids, entertainment is pretty much the number one goal. Get them interested because its funny. Or because its all about action. Or young love. Or Vampires. Or magic.

When you run out of books - say a series only has 7 books and they've read them all, where do you go?

You can't hand most 10 year-olds a 600 page Harry Potter book, and they might not be care about reading the Summer Vacation of Barbie.

That's where this range books arrived and made reading compelling for young boys and girls alike.

Choose Your Own Adventure

Have you ever read a book and wished that it had an alternate ending? Well imagine a book with 10 different endings. And each ending depends on a decision you make.

You're at the edge of the cliff

1. If you jump off into the river below, turn to page 87
2. If you start climbing down the cliff, turn to page 74

These books gave control of the action (adventure) to the young reader. And started a multi-million dollar market for interactive books worldwide. Where else could you read a book 10 times and have a different story every time! Of course the best part of the book was - you were the star. So you were not just reading, you were LIVING the book! Genius!

In the early days of computer games, you could play on your black and white TV with a simple controller, usually a joystick or a wheel. They had simple driving games, Pong, and eventually Space Invaders and PacMan. You could practice at home if you had a console, then go to public places on machines where others could watch and be amazed at your skill.

But they were primarily one-person games, or you could alternate turns in the same game. The games had a pattern, and if your memory was good enough you could plan your strategy and be patient to beat your opponents score.

Then some games got clever and let you play against someone in real time. Mortal Combat, boxing, punching, kicking and fighting games had two players at the console. Bigger and bigger crowds would gather as the winner takes all process let teenagers spend their days at the arcade. Of course they refined their skill in front of an audience. And spent a lot of money!

But when home consoles came in with Nintendo 64, and Atari, people had to play by themselves, or with one other person. Usually a younger brother or sister unless a friend came over to play.

And kids got bored once they mastered the game through endless repetitions, or had no worthy opponents remaining.

In the 2000's, XBOX came out with the ability to play online, over the internet, with people anywhere in the world. XBOX Online plugged into your home internet, and you could compete with people around the world. Nintendo's Wii and Playstation soon followed. They allowed you to collaborate in multi-player combat mission games, or race each other in Mario Kart.

This seamless transition to interactivity with total strangers bonded by a love of a game, turned the games industry into a multi-billion dollar industry. Your home is now linked to the world of people just like you and you can play .... Forever.

Before we talk about how you can use this principle in your presentations, here's some examples from TV.

Big Brother

More than 10 years ago, a hand-picked group of strangers were flung into a house together. 24/7 the public was able to watch their every move through cameras installed around the house. Sleeping, eating, showering and reading, playing games and interacting with each other. Sound boring?

The contestants were deliberately chosen for their personalities which would conflict with some and attracted to others.

Mostly they were extroverts happy to show themselves to the world. And watch the world did. Big Brother became a ratings success and the TV concept duplicated around the world for more than ten years in dozens of countries.

The Amazing Race

A cancer survivor who had battled and survived. Then he realised that his bucket list of places to go and things to do was still long, went out and did those things. After achieving his list, he created a mini-version of this as a competition. He got sponsors, a TV crew, and offered the chance for 12 teams of 2 people to race around the world. To do some of the bucket list challenges he himself had done, and for the thrill of competition - one couple would win a million dollars. Phil Keoghan's bucket list has never been so public and adopted by others so successfuly. The concept has continued expanding around the world and has been adapted by companies wanting a challenge of their own on a local scale.

Idol

Talent shows have always been popular. Judges in small towns across the country have discovered incredible talent that have become the musicians we know and love today. But when you have 50,000 people audition for 200 places, and televise the auditions its a new world. The whole auditioning and callback process live on TV, with 3 judges giving their support and acid feedback. We can all see the reactions of the aspiring artist , and then we the public get to vote on who goes further in the competition…. We're hooked.

Reality TV has changed our lives. Big Brother, The Amazing Race, and American Idol (X Factor, Australia's got Talent, The Voice). They all get the concept of involvement or interaction with their audience.

In Big Brother the voyeuristic audience at home made their judgements, and voted on who would stay and who would go from the house. Based on who they liked. Who they felt a connection to. Who they felt they would be friends with.

In the Amazing Race, the competitors stimulated the travel dreams of millions of TV watchers. We all wished we could make wine in Tuscany, go Ziplining in the Amazon, Climbing the Sydney Harbour Bridge or fly away anywhere in a plane!

Talent shows allow the people at home to experience amazing first time performances. And then give direct support with Twitter and text messages to vote for their favourites. These shows helped strangers one day become stars then next. When you hear them on the radio the day after they won the competition you know the format works.

Reality TV brought interaction to our lives through our nature to compete, barrack for our favourites, and the power of our vote.

Getting involved with your audience is something that the TV producers understood. That the authors of the Choose Your Own Adventure books understood. That the Computer Games industry understood.

So you need to understand it too, and integrate it into your speaking strategy.

When you speak to an audience, there can be the feeling that you are the only one there.

Having great stories and being enthusiastic, passionate, and entertaining is great. But if it's all about you, your audience will get bored.

It's important for you to look at your talk and plan to involve your audience. Every presentation can include a level of interactivity or audience involvement.

Let's look at some of the ways you can get your crowd into your talk.

Questions

In my first book (Master the Art of Public Speaking Volume 1) we talked about the many ways that you can use questions in a presentation. I want you now to think about specific strategic questions that will aid you in getting your audience involved.

Yes or No.

Questions that get one of two answers are useful in many ways. Sometimes you want to build your presentation up to get a series of agreements. Or negative agreements.

"You can see the benefit of saving $1138 per year in electricity?"
"Does it make sense to keep the solar panels on your roof active?"
"So will we increase the number of panels to save you even more?"

All these have a logical "Yes" to them. This builds your momentum in a sales pitch, or in getting agreement to the final decision.

You don't always get the sale on the first Yes. Cementing in the agreement can be a powerful sales tool.

If you get a Yes it can also verify that people are listening and what you are saying is making sense.
If things don't make sense, you confuse them or are unclear, and they don't continue to listen. Don't go past confusion, or you will never get the outcome you desire.

"Do you like looking at how much money is in your bank right now?" No

No can be the perfect response in a talk. You don't always need "Yes" to get to a positive outcome. There are a lot of people that say negative responses from your audience lead to poor results. But that is not my experience. No is a great reminder to them of what they are thinking. And if they are thinking it, I believe you should hear it from them. Thoughts lead to words, and when your audience speaks them they are more powerful than just thinking them.

Thoughts, Words, Actions. You want the action? Then verbalise the thought.

You must remember that questions are a specific tool. And should only be used at certain times.

Don't annoy your audience with 9 questions in a row that demand a "Yes". Thats manipulation.

Don't make them answer yes if they don't naturally do it. They will be thinking it. Learn a better way to ask your question so you can get them involved.

Activities

While used most commonly in training presentations, the use of an activity in a talk can be good almost any time.

The activity needs to be relevant to the topic, and short enough that you get your point, and can move on. You don't want to have to make a paper plane for 10 minutes as you'll lose all momentum.

Simple activities can be:

- Encouraging them to raise their hand as a response
- Waving to them and getting the wave back (instructional)
- Clapping because of the power of your point, or after having a volunteer speak
- Laughing - because you're funny - on purpose or by accident (which you design on purpose)
- Repeating after you key statements to reinforce them
- Standing up to stretch and other physical activity
- Reflection and thinking
- Writing activities
- Writing lists
- Creating a plan
- Calculations

- Handouts
- Drawing a picture
- Making a map
- Partner activities
- Reviewing material
- Research
- Role Plays
- Discussing Case Studies or examples
- Strategising
- Competitions
- Games
- Using a physical object such as a ball, balloon, feather, or object relevant to your talk like money. Pass it around and make it the centre of the discussion.

Now we've discussed the concept of interaction, let's move on to specific strategies you can use in your talk.

CHAPTER SIX
Interactive Activities

Building Stronger Rapport

When teaching something for the first time, I will use a 5 minute period of reflection and creation with my audience. I encourage them to have a pen and paper. After outlining my first key point or strategy, they take part by writing notes. This interaction sets the tone of the rest of the talk as I repeat the process many times in a 3 hour workshop or talk. The notes taken then are the action steps based on the talk. So they are often more valuable than the notes they take throughout the main body of the presentation.

Reflection where you only use silence to think is bad. Unless its no more than 10 seconds. People think pretty fast. If you give them five minutes to think about anything, they finish that in less than one. Then they go back on their phones checking facebook and email and messenger.

Time is elastic. This is a principle that I use in all time-sensitive presentations. What feels like a long time when you are speaking, goes fast for the audience. But blank space. Silence. That seems to take forever for the crowd.

Give people 10 seconds to think of things. Their instinctive response happens in about 1 second anyway, it just allows time for everyone to catch up.

Then encourage people to share what they have reflected on.

The best presentations are always two-way, and if you have created the opportunity for them to speak, respect what they say by listening.

The person that speaks up is usually going to be the voice for others thinking the same thing. For you it's great feedback to incorporate as your presentation continues.

Handouts

Every presentation can benefit by giving people something to hold in their hands. After all, if they are holding a sheet about you in their hands, they aren't on their phones!

Handouts can be flyers, business cards, objects, or magazines - but you want them to be at least the size of a full sheet of paper. That way they can sit it on top of their notepad or ipad and see it.

If it's a sales sheet, you want that in their peripheral vision while you speak.

As your speaking continues, the value in what you say increases, and the desire to get what you are selling increases too.

Handouts can also be great when they are interactive tools themselves. You can use instructional powerphrases to get people to fill in their name, numbers, emails, and more. As the speaker, you hold the power. So use it to encourage them to participate. Even when it's as simple as filling in a form to help you.

Sample handouts include:

Build your database - with name, email, phone number to register for your special free offer

Pre-fill an order form - for what you're selling

Calculate savings or earnings - good for investments, insurance, or income proposals

Reduce the price on a Sales offer by physically crossing it out and writing the new price

Physical Activity

I attended many presentations, bootcamps, workshops and seminars in the 90's and 2000's. As a result, I've seen every possible form of physical activity used as an interactive tool.

Getting your body moving is great, and can be as simple as standing up and stretching. Sometimes a speaker may encourage the audience to talk briefly.

If it's been one-sided talking from the stage for a while, it's a nice break. Those people that want to talk and releases some of the energy can. It also gets those thoughts out of their head so they don't build up.

Advanced strategies for physical interaction include massages, trust falls, singing circles and more. I will discuss those further in the Trainers Guide To Success in a future book.

For the everyday speech or presentation, keep to the simple forms of interaction, so you stay on track and on time with your talk!

Staying in control of your talk is something your audience is judging you on, even if they are having a good time. Nothing is worse than the speaker who has to rush. Worse still is a speech that finishes without completing all the slides or all their key points because they went off track.

Research

Thanks to the internet being in the hands of just about every member of your audience, you have to be careful not to make bold statements. Challenge the wrong audience and they will correct you with Google.

But if you plan, you can use this same addicting habit audiences have for your advantage.

For example, if you quote the unemployment statistics for 2012. You might ask the audience "Who here would be able to look up the same statistics for last year?" This lets the audience know that you are aware there are more up-to-date data available. The local 'expert' is going to get some kudos by looking it up on their phone right there and then, and share it with everyone.

Of course the ultimate fun for a speaker is to set a challenge that everyone can compete in. Usually this will be finding an obscure fact or statistic that is buried deep on a wikipedia page or inside content rich websites.

Think about what you could do for an internet research challenge in your next talk. They need to find the result in less than 30 seconds, otherwise it could drag on and on and lose the impact of the activity.

But while they do the exercise, you can have a drink, cough, catch your breath, or revisit your notes. And no-one will notice. In a longer presentation, you can give them 5 minutes for the task, in a team, and take a quick bathroom break. Use the internet to your advantage. Better still, make the task to find something on your own website!

Volunteers

There are always people who will volunteer to come up on stage and get involved. In every audience. In the last book we talked about front row people being always willing to get involved and interact. While useful to know, you cannot underestimate the strategic impact.

Involving a volunteer gives the audience a voice. Someone that is now a part of the action and part of the talk. They will shape the memories people have of this day. And even though 80% of the audience will never volunteer, they do imagine that it is them up on the stage. They think of what they would have done, they hear themselves speaking, and they experience it in an out-of-body kind of way.

Knowing this, you have to choose your volunteer well, and know exactly what you are planning to have them do. Don't just grab the first hand that goes up, they may be the least qualified, and have no value. Then you just have to repeat to make your point.

Please remember. You only bring up a volunteer to make a point. You want to illustrate using a 'live' person and show that what you are saying in theory will work.

I like to lead up to asking for a volunteer by describing a difficult skill like telling a joke. Talk about how many people get it wrong. Give a bit of theory on how it would work better. Give some examples of my own, then some examples of jokes from other people.

Then ask for volunteers. The harder the topic, the fewer the volunteers. If you've got this far in your talk, reading your crowd you should know. In the leadup to asking for a volunteer, you should have a fair idea who already laughs at your jokes, who is on your side and involved. That's the one you want. Not the front row person who is eager, but not yet skilled enough to think on their feet and give you a good outcome.

Because you want this volunteer to succeed, get applause, and show everyone else... YOU CAN DO IT TOO!

Then after the applause dies down, everyone in that audience feels good because they imagined themselves up there.

Multimedia

The use of videos from YouTube, Testimonials, Success Stories and so on are good. They have to be at the right time, and they have to be of a quality that will capture peoples interest.

The problem is most people go overboard when it comes time to play some music or show a video. They dim the lights, get everyone quiet, and they play the video too small and too soft.

If you're going to show a clip - build it up! Keep the lights on, turn up the volume, and show it! Then transition back to your talk, referencing the media you played, and get feedback from your audience.

It won't be perfect, but your audience isn't sitting in their home theatre with surround sound. They're watching your presentation that you're in control of. The video is a tool. The talk is the key.

Also, don't rely on the internet to load and buffer your video. You'll lose precious seconds. Or minutes if it doesn't load at all. Always have the hard copy in your presentation so if the internet goes down, you aren't relying on it. Backup, have spares, on USB and on your hard drive. Of your entire presentation if that's how you're delivering it.

Try to incorporate at least 4 interactive parts to your presentation. It's impact will last longer than just you standing there talking. You'll be memorable, and people will have something tangible to take home with them.

But you don't want people to think that 'being you' is impossible. This next chapter will show you the way to be more approachable immediately to any audience.

CHAPTER SEVEN
ImPerfection

In the audience you want a good person on the stage. Someone who comes out and tells you what you want to hear. They look great, their words are clear, they present facts with confidence. They seem to have answers for everything, it almost seems too good to be true.

If someone has lots going wrong on stage, that can be distracting and cringe-worthy.

But if someone is too 'perfect' it can be just as annoying. They can appear to have a level of success or expertise or intelligence that we can never hope to match. So we feel worse than when the 'disaster' speaker is on stage. At least we know we could have done better.

Fact: Unfortunately, most audiences are cynical. Prone to a bit of disbelief until we can create the connection that makes what we are saying believable. And what we are often hearing in our heads is this judgement when people start speaking and they appear over-confident.

You know that you don't trust slick car salesman or people who over-promise before they know you.

This is why people are often afraid to stand up and speak, because there are so many judgements taking place.

How crazy is it - if we look too good, we are still going to be judged. Just after we read about getting our connection through interactive exercises! Now you're hearing that you shouldn't be too good!

Which way is it? Let's continue with this line of thought for just a few minutes.

When you are listening to presentations, either speeches, trainers or lectures, it is easy to look at them and judge.

I know that I've said before that we all judge. And we judge the person even more than the material! After all it's a bit harsh, looking at a speaker's clothing and assuming they don't know what they're talking about.

But we're judgemental by nature.

I believe it has something to do with comparing ourselves to others, and looking to improve ourselves. We improve by choosing people to judge where we know we can win.

We never choose the big guy to fight, because we know we would lose

We never choose an equal, because thats a 50:50 decision at face value. In fact they may have fighting training, or be fitter, or more flexible, or more intelligent.
We always pick the guaranteed win.
Some would call this the path of least resistance.
This decision making process is the opposite to what we have to do when we are learning.

Let's look at a few examples, and see what you think.

A woman comes out to speak, after an introduction explaining her high IQ. We hear about her three doctorates, her four children's careers - 2 doctors, one teacher and an artist. Her charity work volunteering at the soup kitchen.

A young man comes out to speak with one arm, bald, and his introduction talks about his struggle with learning English as a child. His cancer, and his parents both being killed in a car accident.

A teenager stands up to speak with her head held up high. She is loud, direct, almost bossy. Pointing her finger at people when she speaks, her introduction was all about her being the daughter of a politician.

A man strides to the stage in suit and tie. With a distinguished voice, and real charisma and presence. His introduction talks about how many millions of dollars he is worth.

Every one of these people creates a reaction in the audience.

The woman? Wanted to speak about charity, but we judge her because we think she doesn't have a real life. Its too perfect.

The young man? We have pity, and we cannot help but listen to him and feel for him.

We judge the teenager because of her parents.

And we all take the financial advice of someone who looks like his life is in control.

Thats the first impression. The most important one.

But something else is just as important for us as speakers to get our image right, and line it up with our introduction and our first word. We need to make sure everyone stays listening to us.

And the secret is imperfection.

We have to be a little less perfect than we think.

I mention in the chapter on "Umms and Ahhs" in my first book how distracting they are. When you sit in the audience you can be so focused on the distraction, that you miss the entire talk! It happens on the TV when Talk Show hosts interview actors and actresses. It happens when politicians get questions they aren't prepared for. Think of the "Great Debates" you've watched in the past when the question wasn't on the original list. Even the most polished performers struggle.

But what I didn't share before is realising that its not always a bad thing to have something wrong with your presentation. To not be the 100% perfect Ken or Barbie doll when you go on stage.

Most presentations only meet about 30% of their potential, because of their lack of preparation.

Speakers lack practice out loud and never got the feedback to help them improve.

I think you should aim somewhere between 90 and 95.

It's time to learn to build in some imperfection

Side Note: If your talk is only at 30% of your potential, you have a lot of 'perfecting' to go. You don't need to work on making it any less perfect or effective. People are already judging you, and that's why you're reading this book. To raise your numbers!

How do we apply this to the examples before?

- If the woman with the High IQ came out and said she failed her first year at University, it humanises her, helps us realise she isn't perfect.
- If the young man tells a joke about how he always said please instead of thank you while learning English, we would like him. Then we focus less on his disability.
- And the young girl? If she's speaking in front of a group of strangers, don't use your parents name! And let the audience know in advance that her dynamic speaking is because of her passion for protecting young girls from abuse.

- The Gentleman speaker could share the story of the 'one that got away' in his relationships. We can empathise that you can't have every area of your life perfect.

You have to construct your image and your style, with these ways to help more people build rapport with you and want to listen. They will approach you after a talk if you are more human, and less superhuman.

No-one can read your mind. They don't realise any of your faults, when you are so busy focusing on your strengths. You have to spell them out.

It makes you human. It makes you normal.

If you don't appear to have anything wrong with you, it's harder to trust you. No-one can be that perfect.

I am going to assume you already prepared with your talks. That you could do them blindfolded. You've memorised the talk and your gestures and pauses. You tested your jokes and it's going to go off according to plan. And you've given the talk 5 or 6 times.

Then you might be ready to insert some imperfection.

Let's review the principles around why people attend talks.

As an audience, we come to sit at the feet of people who know more more.
Are more intelligent.
Are more knowledgeable.
Have studied more
Have made more money
Have what we want.

And because they have what we want, we need to remove our fears and insecurities. They aren't better than us, we should instead see them as an expert and take the time to respect them and listen.

We want to learn, we want to get value from the presentation.

But we don't want them to not know too much more than us.

Thats where the professional presenter understands his audience well. Based on that knowledge, they remove perfection from their performance.

Planned Imperfection.

If our brain is finding someone to be too perfect, we won't listen to them. Our ego will back up and find things wrong with them that may or many not be true. And we won't get the value from their presentation.

If there is something you notice out of place like a small stutter, stumble, or lisp. A piece of clothing that doesn't quite look like the latest fashion. Then you will realise that the speaker isn't perfect. You accept them and then you overlook it if the talk is good.

I'm suggesting that you plan something obvious.

How do you build these into your talk? With as much precision as you prepared your talk in the first place.

Let's look at a few areas that we could work on. And then you can choose the ones that you want to build into your talk.

Know-it-All

Nobody likes the person that knows everything. Even in the age of smartphones and Google, Siri, and Wikipedia, some mystery is nice.

So even if you do know the answer all the time, when an audience asks, its ok to not know everything. In fact its is useful to let the audience discover someone in the crowd with them knows the answer. Which you can agree with or just acknowledge them.

Most people distrust the person who has to answer everything. Especially if they make it clear that their answer is the only answer, and the right answer.

I remember as a kid, people commenting on my confidence. It's probably why I like helping other people to this day. But I did have a backhanded compliment given to me on my 10th birthday. I received a poster that stated:

"Those of you that think
you know everything,
are annoying to
those of us that do!"

Now as kid I thought nothing of it. But it points to my personality and the way some 10 year old's parents felt threatened or offended by my level of confidence.

It's hard to remove that from someone, so I took the poster at face value as a compliment.

And since then it has reminded me of the way that others will see you. Even if you are a positive thinker, some people don't want to have you in their face, being so 'positive' and 'happy all the time'.

So I keep my opinions around those people to myself, while maintaining my confidence, and my positive attitude.

Failures

We can all relate to failure, mistakes, lost chances. If we are going to share in our talk about our successes, spend some time talking about your failures. You will always get a stronger connection and a better response, by sharing both sides of the story.

Even better still, showing the link between how your failures led to your success.

You will need to take time working on the list of your mistakes - if you're like me you have hundreds - and pick the right one to share.

Everything needs to be relevant to the talk you are giving, the introduction you have, and the lesson you are able to show by sharing this.

It's also important not to share too many mistakes.

The emotion around some failures may affect you. You need to practice telling the story of your failure in front of a mirror. Does it distract you? Do you have anger or sadness? All this will show up when you share it, and you MUST be in control of your emotions when you speak. Otherwise you will lose the impact of both the story and the imperfection.

In fact, the audience will forget your entire talk if the story of your failure is too memorable.

Simple guide for mistakes and failures:

Keep them relatable
Have a point for sharing them
Keep in control of your feelings
Link the failure to a future success

Physical

I had a friend once who wore glasses. He would talk quite close to you in a small group, and as he was tall and I was short, he would be looking down at me. If it was a warm day, his glasses would slide down his nose. So he had to keep pushing them back up.

Which he would do with his middle finger.

Now, I thought he and I were friends, yet for the entire ten minutes of our conversation, all I could focus on was getting the "Bird" up close!

That of course is illogical. But the gesture is still the strongest memory I have of our time together.

You don't want to a reputation for that, so its important instead to come up with something else. Something physical maybe that you do to give an imperfection to your talk.

Here are some suggestions.

Clicking your fingers
Rubbing your nose
Running your fingers through your hair
Rocking back and forwards
Tapping one foot on the floor from time to time
Pointing to emphasise things (not at the same person)
You may have something you already do that your feedback partner has told you about!

Just do them subtly, and make sure you point out to people that you KNOW you are doing it. You could tell them that it happens sometimes when you're nervous. Or when you are telling personal stories.

That builds rapport and humanises you just the way you need to.

Speaking Speed and volume

I speak pretty fast. I learned from some of my early mentors, that if you tell people you're going to talk fast, they're ok with it. And it definitely helps if you are talking with passion or enthusiasm or are wanting to raise the energy of a room. Fast will always win over slow when you are speaking. In context of course with your topic and the emotions that you might be expressing.

When your speaking speed increases, you the only time you might be in trouble is if you have a strong accent. This will usually mean you are a visitor in someone else's country.

I'm familiar with this, speaking in Russia, Hungary and Romania recently with translators. Even in countries where everyone understands English as their second language they often still use translators.

My translator needs to be able to understand me, so I take my time getting faster. When I am confident they have my style, I get faster. They do that by listening to how and what I'm saying. The faster they're translating, the faster I can go.

Explain the imperfection of fast talking to your audience. Say it's because you're so enthusiastic and passionate. Or just have so much to share you can't wait to tell it all.

They will see that enthusiasm, and no-one was ever disliked as a speaker that was fast and enthusiastic.

How about the alternative to high-speed?

If you speak slow, too slow, people will go into a hypnotic trance and fall asleep. It's hard to get your message across if your audience has lost interest, or drifted into daydreams!

You can use slowness in key moments. Especially when you are telling a deep story. Where emotions are strong. Thats not a weakness, thats a strength.

For your imperfection, it's better to have a lot of variety. Where possible have something unique that people notice. Then you can discuss it with them and together you have the permission from the audience to be different.

Clothing style and Fashion

Well I have a great example here. I spoke for two years in a shiny silver suit. And I loved it. But I told people it was a wedding suit that I wanted to get more wear out of. And they would always smile and laugh. Because of that, I knew I had a way to make the imperfection of only owning one suit at the time, a feature of my talk. And one that people would not forget.

I knew everyone would have an opinion. Sharing a story about it, made it ok. Even if they still judged it.

In a recent tour of Romania, I had just left the USA and retired my black leather formal shoes. I had sneakers, Hiking boots, and Loafers to choose from for my talk.

So I wore the hiking boots.

They were light yellow, with strong yellow soles. My suit was Charcoal Blue. So of course when I went up on stage in front of 400 people, I knew that some people in the audience would notice this. It could affect them, focusing on the boots and not the talk. So I made a point of telling a story about the snow and the weather, and how I liked to prepare for anything, so I put the boots on 'just in case'.

The audience laughed, I saved myself having to buy a pair of shoes for the one day. And I had an imperfection that I was wearing in case anyone started thinking I was too perfect. I didn't.

I don't recommend being perfect in your clothes, except for at your wedding.

And if you do bring in something that is out of place - like wearing red shirt and red tie - make a comment about it. Don't take yourself too serious. And be sure to keep using the same combination if it gets results.

So don't worry about being perfect. It's hard enough to get good enough to need a lot of imperfection. But look at your personal inventory and take advantage of the natural aspects of your talk that can help you to 'keep it real'.

Audiences will connect with you, listen to you, and you'll get your message across.

Now let's go back to one of my favourite ways to get your talk off to a flying start. Applause, cheering and the smile of your audience!

CHAPTER EIGHT
How to get a standing ovation

A seminar attendee from London reminded me recently of something he learned at my seminar about applause.

He said learning how to give a standing ovation was the most powerful thing he got. Because now everytime he hears an introduction, he is the first to clap, and after a few seconds, he stands and claps even louder.

The speaker smiles, the clapping of the audience gets louder, and because most people are followers, they do what the he is doing. They stand too, and clap as loud as they can.

A few whistles, a few cheers, and the speaker is feeling on top of the world.

Thats when you give you best work. When the audience is on your side.

So what do you need to do? Wait for my seminar? No!

Plant people in the audience who are going to stand up and clap!

Now if that doesn't work, or isn't possible, you need to train people to give you a standing ovation. Where do you do that?

In your introduction.

99% of the time, when you give the Master of Ceremonies your written introduction, they will follow it word for word.

Of course I don't like to leave that to chance either. I prefer to have them read it out loud to me, and read it to themselves a few times, practicing key areas of emphasis.

The magic last sentence on your introduction should be:

"So ladies and gentlemen, please stand up and give a big welcoming round of applause to your next speaker, Coach Mark Davis!"

This is a great time for you to realise the power of the stage. When you tell the audience what to do, because you're in charge, they follow!

The Master of Ceremonies is already standing and clapping. Then a few people in the front row stand up, making it easy for everyone behind them to follow.

And in an audience of 10 or an audience of 1000… this works well everytime.

The energy of a crowd standing, applauding, as they say your name… it's a great way to start.

But I would like to show you the contrasting option.

If you just walk up on stage without an introduction, you are starting with low energy. You have a quiet, anxious room, with all the questions and concerns about you still in peoples minds. As well as them thinking about their outside lives.

When you walk up with them cheering and clapping you have already won half the battle. Now they want you to succeed because they have just done the cheering they would do at the end of your talk.

So to get the same applause at the end, you encourage your host to walk up on stage after you finish and say thank you. Then while that applause is still going, the host waves their arms up and down. And says, "Come on, stand and let Mark know how much we appreciate him coming tonight. That was great, Thank you Mark!"

Those that were applauding first now stand and cheer and holler and whistle and clap louder. For them its a great chance to get out of their seats, and to stretch, and to release some energy in the form of noise. Especially when they have been quiet for minutes or even hours.

Work with your audience, but plan what you want them to do.

Now I know you might be sitting there saying to yourself... "That will never work. That's manipulation, people can see through it."

Really?

Everything is manipulation

And people want to you to lead them when they are in an audience. They wouldn't be there without wanting something to change. To learn something, to have someone sell an idea to them. To get new choices in their life about what to believe and what to think.

Because when you are a student, you are there to be led by the teacher. And today, that's you on the stage. So lead!

Everything is moving towards people either liking you or hating you. You have to use whatever is at your disposal to get them to like you, or it's pointless standing in front of them. You won't get through and your message will fall on deaf ears. And no-one and nothing will change.

So use this principle and see what happens.

The worst that can happen is you get a few people standing and they clap a bit more. It will always be more than if you just say, "Please welcome our speaker…"

So using this concept, let's explore other ways you can lead your audience into the direction you want them to think, speak, or act.

Now we're going to look at Collective Psychology, Scarcity, Breaking the Ice, and Money. All are ways to get the audience thinking with you and following you.

Collective Psychology

"No man is an island."

This is true in an audience particularly when you are asking questions from the stage that need an answer. When many people answer a question with the same answer, it's a way of collecting them all together. They change from being a room full of individuals, to an individual room. Even if they just think it, when every person in a room of 2500 says "Yes" you have great power in that room.

People begin to think together, and when you present a new concept for them to think about , they start to respond the same way.

You might want a negative response, so you can ask a question that gives a collective "No!" Or you can illustrate injustice and ask "Is that OK?" Again, the "No!" will be universal.

Be careful using the power of universality when you are presenting a concept, an idea, a product or service for the first time. You should understand what most of the questions or objections are going to be. And then you ask the audience about that.

For a travel company, you could say something like this.

"You might be asking yourself, why would I use that travel portal when I can book my travel at the airlines website?"

You tap into what you know people are thinking. And the nods from the audience will give you all the direction you need to answer that objection immediately.

When presenting to a board of directors, you might make a suggestion.

"The board has a responsibility to its shareholders to make safe decisions. To not risk the company's reputation. So I encourage you to consider this option."

They know that, but reminding them, gets them all to nod.

You can address the audience as one. And then you can make present your compelling statements. Show your powerpoints, and give a strong closing argument and final comments to just "One" person.

Scarcity

I have read a lot on the theory of abuncance and scarcity in psychology. And after reading many motivational books and attending live seminars. I've also seen it taught and demonstrated at firewalks, and board breaking workshops. I've even trusted myself to fall backwards into the arms of strangers.

People don't want to miss out. And they don't want to be the only one without an experience if everyone around them is doing 'it'.

Because we have a primitive reaction to how much of what is right in front of us, always assuming that it will run out. We worry, because we think there won't be enough.

If there isn't going to be enough, then you have to fight for your piece. You have to get in first. You have to race. To win.

This is a ludicrous belief, for example in the myth that we're all going to starve. If there wasn't enough food and resources on the planet we wouldn't have grown from 5 billion people in the 1980's to over 7 billion today. We are growing as a human population, not shrinking.

Regardless of what may happen in the future, the Scarcity 'program' is running inside people's heads. You should use this to your advantage when you speak.

"There are only 3 coaching slots left"
"This year is almost over so get your tax deductible capital equipment now"
"When you die a Funeral costs at least $6000 so start saving for it now"
"Don't make your family sell your home if you lose your job, get income protection insurance."

Breaking the ice

You can't talk to everyone in the room before your talk starts. But I do recommend talking to as many as possible, especially those in the front row. Find out their names, their job, their title, their hobbies. What they like to do in their spare time. Discover the talker, find out who likes to volunteer. Who thinks they're beautiful and who thinks they're smart.

You can use all this when you get on stage.

Comedians do it all the time but make a lot of the stuff up for laughs. Or twist it to make normal everyday people seem funny.

Trainers and Teachers know their students because they get to know them over time, 3hr, a day, a year.

You need to find out who they are BEFORE you speak.

This is what happens next.

When you're talking, you can reference some of those people in the front row. Use their names, their jobs, their goals.

Link your talk to their hobbies and their interests.

And watch how your audience responds.

They become more interactive. Because they see the relationship between the speaker and the crowd. The connection. The smiles, the nodding, the laughter, the link is strong.

And because of Scarcity, they don't want to miss out on it. So they begin to connect the same way. They raise their hand more. Nod more, Answer questions out loud.

The effect ripples from the front of the room to the back, and the faster you use these people to your advantage, the faster the ripple. Then you have the audience... in the palm of your hand.

Money

We'll discuss money in the chapter on Numbers, but I want you to use Money in your opening session because of one key reason.

Money is emotive. It's the thing people hold onto the most because its what they value as a measure of their security.

When they hear you talking about money, it is always better when you focus on having more, growing the money you have. Building on investment is better than spending more.

Nobody believes in others sharing wealth. They believe its hard to get money and to keep it. So you have to follow those beliefs if you are going to sell to them an idea that will need any of their money.

Money is emotive because people believe they can't live without it. So they always want more, to be sure they have enough to survive.

They don't quit jobs because of it. They don't risk it unless they are sure of the return and the security.

You can work with the topic of money, and in the next chapter it'll make more sense how to use it effectively.

CHAPTER NINE
The numbers are the key

When you speak you have to use all the tools available to get your message across. One of the most effective is the use of numbers.

We're going to talk in this chapter about Odd numbers, Exact numbers, and key numbers like 10, 7, 3 and 2.

Why numbers are important comes back to the simple need for the brain to find order amongst chaos. To have a sense of time amidst a sea of words. To give memorable phrases. Numbers help us to do this. And when it comes to money, everything is measured with numbers.

The Top 10

David Letterman of the "Late Show" loved - among other things - doing a particular piece of light entertainment.

"Tonight's Top Ten"

It was usually a countdown of jokes made about someone or something in the news that day.

This taps into one of the skills mentioned earlier in the book, remembering where you are and being relevant to your audience to build a connection.

Politicians were often used as the raw material.

Especially if they had done something silly like winning an election, getting shot by a colleague, or wearing silly clothes.

Similar stories and jokes would be in the opening monologue, but then the highlights would be in the countdown from 10 to 1. Building along the way with mini punchlines and anecdotes. Then the number one joke, the band played, the crowd went wild, and the segment was over with laughs all round.

He did it every night of his show! It must work.

But why does the Top Ten work so well?

A Top Ten gives laser focus. Ten items on the one topic!

You can stop worrying about everything else that is going to happen on the show. It's a 2 minute segment, on one topic, and it is 'light' too. No heavy concepts.

Which was also important for the show, which started between 10:30 and 11pm every night. It's not the time to be making people think too hard. People are settling in before bed for some entertainment after a long day.

An example of using ten in the action plan of a Success Seminar talk I used to give on mastering new skills. Ten is a good length of list, and its a nice round number. Our decimal system is ten. It's how our numbers work, and we are comfortable with it.

For example:

Things to do This Week: My Top Ten

- Start every new task with a mentor or coach - you'll find one just by asking anyone who already has expertise in the are you need help in.

- Find out the reward or payoff for a new project, and you know there is a fair and reasonable reward for the risks you'll have to take.

- Call in all the support you can from your trusted friends.

- Take a speed-reading course or learn to touch-type. You'll get your thoughts down faster, and consume more information.

• Be aware that there are always more succesful people than you, and always more losers than you. It's a journey.

• Hold your head high when you're trying something new. In most cases, the act of beginning gives you learning experiences that are priceless. Most people never begin.

• Learn from people you like, who make you feel good about yourself when you leave their training, seminar, books or tapes. Avoid people who make you feel wrong.

• Surround yourself with confident people who will give you tips on increasing your speed of learning.

• Realise you don't have to do everything that comes your way. Sometimes it's the deals you don't do that make you the most money. There are more fish in the sea. Don't be pressured into anything.

• Mentor other people, to teach them what you've learned. You'll make it easier for them- teaching through the generations is our way of

making the world a better place..
And pick a book, a newspaper, anything - and try reading a bit of it upside down. Not the whole thing, just a few lines. You might just be surprised.

So we can apply this concept in our speaking. The concept of a limited number of points, and sticking to it.

Getting their attention with 7

Most people can only focus on 5-7 things at once with their conscious mind, and we don't like to go wider than that. If you work on these numbers, you can divert the focus from the narrow "Top Ten" and outline more ideas.

If you have "7 steps to Success" and each step takes 10 minutes, you don't just have a 70 minute talk. You have a 70 minute attention span. Because one thing the human mind loves to do is make order in things, and follow the order of things. It knows that sooner or later they'll hear all 7 steps. No-one wants to miss a step, so they stay alert, paying attention, writing notes, and getting engaged.

By the way, you would never jump from tip number 3 to tip number 8.. It would confuse people. Even though they don't need a set order, the mind loves the order of a countdown. It gets excited, and it keeps us engaged and interested. Follow the logic of this concept and watch your audiences interest in you grow.

Three

This is why 3 is a popular number. When you use past, present and future in your examples you are using the power of three. Three gives options allowing you to not feel like it has to be one or the other. Instead, the third choice gives us a feeling of power over our decisions. Even though psychology always tells us that we will choose the middle option when given three choices, most of the time.

Cars are sold to us in threes. The cheap one, the expensive one, and the one in the middle, just at the top end of what we can afford.

Food comes in three categories, the Budget brand, the Known brand, and the Premium brand. It depends on our values, our ego and our budget which way we go.

Three Wise Men, Three Blind Mice, Movie Trilogies. The Holy Trinity, Proverbs, sayings, and quotations. Jokes too - "Three guys walk into a bar, an Australian, an Englishman and an Irishman"

You can use Three in many ways when presenting on the stage.

If you were a politician, suggesting project options at a private meeting:

"We can build a road across that river with a Bridge that will cost $2M, and get 200,000 cars a day across it. Or we can build a road that goes around the river and uses the existing bridge. That will slow traffic on that bridge and only allow an extra 40,000 cars a day across and the others will catch public transport. Or we can do nothing, and have voters banging on the door till we do!"

If you were a music teacher presenting to a students mother:

"I've given Alice the choice of three new pieces of music to practice. One at the same level of her skill, one that is a little bit harder, and one that is quite challenging and will take a while to master. Which do you want to choose?"

Or if you were a Car Salesman, showing an 18 year old the choices for their first car:

"Well the safe option is this Volvo, its done 273,000 km and has only had one owner.

"Or this brand new sedan with 17 compartments and great fuel economy.

"Or this convertible which was just traded in this morning, and will let you drive around with the top down so everyone can see you."

The variety in choice with three is great as it seems to give control to people, when in fact it gives them two choices. One is to change nothing, and the other is to grow and move forward. How far forward is a variation on the same theme.

Most innovators and entrepreneurs use three as their decision making number.

They are then choosing projects between one level of risk that is low and one that is higher. The options are always available, but only rarely used. The third option is to stay still and do nothing.

Tennis players do this now, getting three balls before they serve, choosing the best two out of the three. It's a habit that annoys some in the audience, but when they choose the 'right' one and serve an ACE! Everyone forgives them.

You can use three in this powerful way used by successful presenters.

Make your point, usually with a story, or case study.

Make your point again with a variation on the story to show that it isn't just a one-size approach.

Then make your point once more with a universal example showing the reason why its such a good point!

For more on this technique, see the chapter on Repetition.

TWO

When you use Before and After, you are using the number two. Two is a simple decision based number.

Yes or No.

High or Low.

Accept or Refuse.

Giving people opposites, or simple choices using two, helps move things forward.

The most common is Yes and No. When you ask questions on stage you can use this to find yourself directing the audience through their responses. Yes and No give you the power of instruction, demanding an answer to move on. Used well, this will get you to your key points, and have the audience feel like they helped shape the presentation. This is one of the reasons we use questions as discussed in my first book.

Two simplifies presentations, and is often easier than the challenges that Three presents.

I like to reference a friend of mine, Tom "Big Al" Schreiter, who likes to train using the power of two in his talk on Personalities. You can find his books at www.BigAlBooks.com.

A sentence that he uses to help audiences make decisions about their personal style is this:

"There are two types of people."

This simple presentation sentence helps the entire audience - of 5 or 5000 - give themselves a label. They will be one of these two types.

It simplifies the concept in the audience's mind because they don't have to consider being one of 24 different types of people. Even though their intention is good, a speaker who gives too many options confuses the audience. And they are confused, they don't act.

There are two types of people. Those who agree with the above sentence, and those that don't.

Black and White. That's what the power of two does for you, it removes the grey areas. Helps you clarify.

In the chapter earlier we used the example of the successful books, "Choose Your Own Adventure." When the time came to make a decision, they always gave two options.

For a 7 or 8 year old reading the book, and having more than two choices, confusion would win. Going left or right, through the waterfall or off the cliff, holding on or letting go. Two rules.

You can also use the power of Two here:

Yes or No
Right or Left
Buy Today or Think about it
Play or Watch
Bat or Bowl
Pitch or Catch
Run or Walk
Stop or Keep Going
Speak or Listen

Limiting peoples choices will always be more effective. It's a faster way to get action and results. Much better than giving too many options and making people choose to do nothing!

Odd numbers

After 20 years in the selling, marketing, and training of people, I have never seen even numbers out perform odd numbers.

Everyone know that a price at 0.99 is a dollar. But still 0.99 is still seen more often.

But if 99 is good, why not 98?

Ask yourself this question.

What number do you trust more. And what number are you more likely to pay?

$19.99, $20.80 or $24.99

Price ceilings and price pressure

Studies show that when you go above $20.00 people have more comfort in a number at the next price ceiling. This is the point at which we think the price is high enough to expect more substance or value for our money. And those numbers jump from $9.99 to $19.99 to $24.99. Then to $39.99 then to $69.99 then $99.99.

The psychology behind this I will leave to psychologists, but it's important to note that all these are odd numbers. The final number in the price is always odd.

It may be a western thing, because Chinese definitely like 8,88,888 and 8888 etc. But in the West, ending in an odd high number, like 7 or 9 sells best.

Look at this number.

$68.42

Its all even numbers, and unless its the total of your shopping basket of groceries, you'll never see it in the retail market.

Just like you won't see $300.86 to buy a TV. $297 is much more likely.

Numbers create reactions in our head that we need to be aware of when we are speaking on the stage.

If we are a real estate presenter, its better to have a house that has an odd size, like 39 square metres or 3900 square feet. 40 or 4000 is less effective, even though the number is bigger.

If we are selling insurance or weightloss, the cost is sold to consumers as a daily or weekly amount. They are usually odd numbers like $2.71 or $15.99

not $2.80 or $16.00. Check your TV next time they advertise.

And if we give one more example to look at the price of airline baggage fees - right now it's usually $25 for the first bag and $15 for the second. Never just $20 even. Odd numbers we believe when big companies sell them to us, and so Odd numbers we should use for our talks.

During the 2000's, people used a lot of 7 in the end of their pricing. It has since reverted to 9 as the favoured number - 19.99, 24.99 or 99.99. Even numbers come in and out of favour. But note they were both odd numbers.

Have a look around next time you're in a TV or Computer store, and even in the supermarket. Chocolate bars at $0.99? Probably when they're on special. TV for $299? $795? $1497? Odd endings all the way.

Exact numbers

People trust odd numbers, doesn't matter why they just do. They are also suspicious of rounded up numbers. So it can be useful for us to have exact numbers when we are referencing statistics or talking about people.

200,000 people sounds like an accurate population? Or 201,445?

Or at the football, the attendance is never put up as 40,000 fans. It's 40,083 or 39,755. No conspiracy theories but it's also much more likely to be a random number than a perfect even number.

We trust the accurate number because we want to believe it. If they are just general numbers, then what else in the talk is just 'general' 'approximate' or 'near enough'.

Specifics build trust and rapport, especially when we have the paperwork to back them up. Studies, reports, statistics all help to build our case for the audience believing us.

And thats how we get our message through

The reason we don't trust most politicians is they speak in general numbers. 24,000 jobs, 100,000 new homes. Half a million education places at university.

Generalities are not trusted.

Think of your own presentation. Are you referencing specifics or vague concepts. How far can you drill down in the statistical proof of what you are doing.

When I was doing Google Adwords advertising, I could measure to 0.001% efficiency. So I could look at every dollar I was spending and make it effective. And justify every decision I made with the return on investment. To the cent. Clients loved it.

What would not have worked was me saying - "Well if you spend about $1000 on ads, you should get about $2000 in sales?"

What works is saying:

"My last client invested $376.01 in January. That got them 420 clicks, 30 enquiries and 3 sales, netting $3003 in sales and returning a 798% return on investment."

Specifics sell.

Whats one of the big decisions we make with chocolate? The % of cocoa. 30%, 50%,70%. The higher the darker the colour, and the more expensive (with quality product) and the better the taste. The higher the antioxidants, the better the endorphin rush.

That's why Lindt puts its Cocoa% on the cover.

Cheap chocolate doesn't. Milk or Dark it just advertises itself as "This is it".

And thats why Lindt can charge 2-3 times as much as regular milk and dark chocolate.

If you are talking about donations to a charity, make sure you announce the exact amount as you are raising it. Every year at Easter, the Good Friday appeal in Melbourne raises funds. They hold a TV appeal for donations for the Royal Childrens Hospital. It's been running for longer than I can remember (since 1931). They currently have a goal of more than 5 Million Dollars to raise in 24 hours of the Appeal.

Across the bottom of the TV screen are the pledges and donations, with the name of the person giving the money.

Every hour, they make a big deal about announcing the donations received so far.

Do you think they say, "About 100 thousand!"

Or "Wow, its a lot of money!!!"

Not, they say "Our 11am total is $367, 411.25!!!! Thank you everyone for your support and looking forward to the next progressive total at 12 o'clock!"

Specifics sell. People believe them. And they are your audience. It helps make buying decisions and makes intangible concepts and ideas real.

Numbers are important for your presentations. Use them well and you can get your message across and build trust and rapport.

And now they like you, you have to get your message to sink in! We do that with Repetition.

CHAPTER TEN
Do it again! And again!

The power of repetition

One of the most amazing performances I ever saw was a training, on VHS video, of Jim Rohn. Philosopher, Mentor, Speaker.

I never got to see him live, so when the chance to watch a video popped up, I leapt at the chance.

The talk was to about 300 people in a hotel ballroom.

He was standing at a lectern, and tapping a pen on the edge of the lectern from time to time as he spoke.

What made him unique and memorable? And why do I quote that talk to this day?

Every time he would complete a key phrase or sentence he would repeat it.

Word for word, as he built his presentation, the talk grew and grew, and then all the key sections had been repeated.

I worked out that he repeated the major point of his talk on "Planning" at least 12 times in the hour long talk.

And here is the magic

Rather than being sick of hearing him share it, the point made more and more sense the more times I heard it.

Like having 8 notes on a piano in a melody that gets catchier and catchier the more you hear the song.

Jim's "Before you start the day, plan the week. Before you start the week, plan the month. Before you start the month, plan the year!" talk grew inside me. Now, more than 20 years later, I still think of that video and the many messages behind it when I am looking to plan for any project.

Presenting an idea - your great idea - is exciting. You feel that you have a philosphy you are passionate about. You believe that it is going to change lives, your concept will save money, your idea will by accepted by everyone that hears it.

But if you only share it once in your entire talk, no-one will remember it. Well…. Maybe 1% of the people.
Every time you repeat your core idea or concept, more people notice it and will remember it.

The more examples you share that tie back to the core idea, the better.

The number of times you say it out loud, increases the audiences retention.

Having it written somewhere

Having it up on a slide.

Having it on a handout in peoples seats.

You won't give away your great idea by repeating it. People don't copy things becaues they are so caught up in their own lives.

You have to repeat to get the impact of your idea.

You have to repeat so you have a chance for people to stop all the other things they're thinking of, and start to focus on you. When you repeat, they think "Wait, I've heard that before, must be important!"

Let's go into detail on the different ways you can use the power of repetition without it becoming annoying for your audience. Instead you can maximise the impact of your talk.

Identical

This is the most common form of repetition.
This is the most common form or repetition.

Exact, word for word duplication of what you said.

There are a few ways you can use this.

Immediately, repeat a sentence that you want people to remember.

They can have time then to write it down, think about it, think about what it means, think about the effects of it, and the impact.

While you are walking around, or reading slides, repeat the key phrase again and again. Two or three times is not unusual or over the top.

In fact, I recommend when you have a great phrase, instruct your audience to write it down.

Warm up to it, give them warning that something important/key/vital is coming. And get them ready to write down this sentence...

This prepares people that the direction of your talk has been taking is leading to a focal point. When you get them to write something down, it will anchor it into their thoughts and into their notepad! (Or iPad.)

When you present the key phrase the first time, wait 5 seconds before repeating it. An example I give in my workshops when discussing the importance of repetition is:

"Oh, this next bit is so important, you'll want to write it down. Grab a pen, steal some paper, and engrave this into your memory forever...

"Never, Give, Up."

(Then I wait 5 seconds)

"I'll say it again, Never Give Up. No matter what is happening, Never Give Up! When people around you say you can't , Never Give Up! When you think you have no energy left, Never Give Up! It's always darkest before the dawn and it can feel like it's so hard to move forward, but.... Never Give Up!"

It looks like a lot of repetition when you write it down, but when you say it out loud it's different.

Take a moment and read that paragraph out loud, with pauses where each sentence stops. And feel the power in your voice, the energy it creates. The way you go up and down with your voice and how that feels so different to just reading it.

It stirs you. Motivates you. Gets you in the belly where your fire burns...

Another example? Let's look at the use of numbers.

I'm standing in front of 150 high school students. About to talk to them about offering a job to work in a hot warehouse and help work in our charity. How do I get their attention? How will I know they are focused on me and wanting to find out more and listen for the whole 20 minutes?

"$4500... $4500... What could you do with $4500? I am looking for about 30 of you that are looking for a job. To make $4500 next year. It'll be hot, It'll be hard work, it's working in a charity and it's one day per week. $4500. One of the students who worked for me last year, I asked what he was going to do with the money he had earned. He was going to buy a car. His friend had spent all the money on cigarettes and alcohol. $4500. What would you do with it?"

The rest of the presentation didn't matter. 45 kids put their name down for work experience and 17 ended up getting a job and making that money the following year.

Repetition helps you in the following ways:

Reinforces the idea as being important
Clarifying the key idea of your talk
Gives you something to come back to again and again through your talk as your theme

Helps you build on one simple concept and make it more and more complex
Locks the focus of the audience for a moment
Prioritises one or more topics

I'm not going to go over it again, it's a great principle you now have to work on incorporating in your talk.

But what's your talk about, we have all these skills and a great talk. But what's the title, and how do we get one that people will love and want to listen to?

CHAPTER ELEVEN
How to design the title of your talk

In the twitter world, you only get 160 characters to get your point across.

For Youtube Videos, the image can set the stage but the caption tells the story

On the front page of a printed newspaper (yes they still exist) the headline is 3-7 words.

Yet this is by design.

Every medium has a different way of making their first impression. Because they want to encourage people to keep paying attention.

Twitter boring? Unfollow.

Facebook status infrequent? Unfriend.

Youtube title unclear? Next!

Newspaper headline not interesting? No sale!

If you don't get your headline or title right, you won't get the point of your message across.

So if you have a 20 minute presentation, they won't listen if your first sentence, or the "Title" of your talk isn't interesting.

There is a lot you can do to get better at writing headlines, and its like writing. You have to start. Just meditating about it won't make it happen.

Inspiration comes often. But genius is in the details of the work we do.

This is never more true than when we are working on designing our talk.

The name of the talk, the headline - the first thing that comes to mind ... is not the one we will end up going with. Because its usually linked to emotion, or to someone elses idea, or maybe IS someone elses idea we read, or saw on TV or heard at another event.

Headline/Title writing is like copy writing. It takes a lot of writing to get the good stuff between the fluff and the 'good ideas'.

Same for the content of the talk or book or presentation.

I know. To write this book it took over 30 hours of solid writing another 20 of editing. I had it reviewed by people around the world, and had to prepare all this in spare time while travelling. Over a period of about 3 months. !

I have studied personal development over many years. It has led me to discover other skills worth having. Copywriting, headline writing, advertising, online pay-per-click marketing, facebook ads and more.

It seems that every day I still keep learning new ways to be better at what I do. But its because I keep wanting to.

I never take for granted that what I know now is all I need. In fact its usually the opposite for me.

I always feel I don't know enough.

So I rely on those before me who have been successful in their field. Those whose ideas challenge me to be a better speaker, entrepreneur, father - whatever the topic I am studying.

I'm going to refer to another great book I read, "Uncommon Marketing Techniques", by Jeffrey Dobkin. It's a red book you'll pick up in the marketing section of big bookshops.

It's called the 100:1 rule.

It's pretty simple, so you'll understand why I keep it that way, and leave you the rest of the page to start getting to work.

"Consider every sentence that is important in your speech. Where the audience's reaction determines your success or failure. Be it the headline, the opening line, the punch line or the conclusion. You have to write that line out 100 times before you choose one to run with."

I'll say it again, in case you think I'm joking.

For every line that's important... write it out, 100 times, before choosing one.

That way you'll know you've done the work required to guarantee your success

I've found that it takes about 4 hours to write out 100 headlines or book titles.

Professionals get paid to do what they're good at.

If a good headline for a speech is worth $10,000, then it's $2500 an hour for writing. A pretty good rate.

If your book sells 50 copies a day and you make $100, every day of the year, the 4 hours you spend is going to bring you $5200.

A bad headline means no-one reads your book or watches your video or reads your newsletter and no-one buys what you're selling.

Because they make up their mind about your speech on the first impression. This is why we talk about it so much including your introduction, Umms and Ahhhs, your body language, the volume you speak at.

So here are a few ideas to help you get to your 100 headlines as the title of your Speech or book.

•   Put adjectives in the title, descriptive, exciting words. Make it bound off the page.

•   Keep it new, hip, innovative, cutting edge. There's enough bad and boring advertising out there. Think about the marketplace today with so much technology and so many ideas, old-school is maybe not the best approach.

- Where is the juicy benefit for your audience? For them, the thing they care about getting from you when you talk?
- What's the thing you're going to teach/discuss/clarify for the audience? How is that different to what they could research online?
- Start it with a How, What, Where, When or Who... to get people listening
- Make their eyes light up - could be shocking or just amazing stories that help

Now lets look at a simple formula for creating a talk. Its not foolproof but you should be able to make a basic presentation by following it. If you miss a section, you may find that the audience also misses the point of your talk. So try to cover everything.

1. First impression.
  a. Headlines, impact, power, getting attention
  b. Connection. Enough emotion in there to make them listen... expecting more of the story
  c. Teaser/Trailer. Just like a good movie, it's the best bits first.
  d. Conclusion. If they stop listening now, it doesn't matter; you've made your point.

2. Body of presentation
    a)   Itemised # of points to cover
    b)   General   introduction/background   of topic/speaker
    c)   Use a story as quickly as possible
    d)   Use a personal story if possible, much more powerful to illustrate point.

    e)   Use 2-3 examples to illustrate your point if it is instructional/how-to, or 2-3 stories of a principle/life skill, eg: importance of time management, show what happens when you do it well and when you don't.

3. Conclusion
    a.   As with first impression, big impact, summarising of points, key emotional trigger points, lessons or principles re-visited
    b.   Repeat key phrases
    c.   Repeat lasting impression/headline from beginning

Finally, lets move on and remind ourselves who we are talking to, and what it is they want.

CHAPTER TWELVE
The Audience Wants What?

What do they want?

There are many different ways to open a talk. Just as there are many different types of speakers. Formal, Casual, Funny, Serious - there is no limit to the categories you can create for yourself as a speaker.

Some people like to use a joke, others like to tell a 20 minute story about themselves. Still others have no preparation, and we know it always ends badly then. Others use examples and some make bold statements.

Whats going to be the best for you?

Let me share why the opening is important, and then we can move into designing and opening that will give you the maximum impact, and have people remember you!

When the audience sits down in any presentation - especially if they paid for it - they have an expectation. They expect a lot of things.

- They want value for their time, so it doesn't feel like they should have been somewhere else.
- They want value for their money - a "Return on Investment" for the money they have exchanged for your knowledge or your secrets or your inspiration.
- They definitely want to be educated to learn something new that they didn't know before. This will give them the strategic advantage over their competition - at work, at home, in the wider marketplace.
- And they want to be entertained. No-one wants to sit for 30 minutes, one, two or three hours - and be bored.

Let's start with entertainment first.

This is always seen by new speakers as humour and jokes. But it has nothing to do with that. People don't go to watch a drama movie at the cinema for the jokes. They go for the chance to leave their world for a moment and enter a new one. To suspend the reality of their lives, and enter a new reality. They see action movies where people jump out of helicopters and have high-speed car chases - not for the jokes. But for the adrenalin, the rush, the heightened sense of awareness as good battles evil, bullets fly back and forth, car tyres scream and the good guys wins.

Entertainment is about giving people an experience that moves them.

So you can do it in a number of ways.

Action/Adventure
Science Fiction/Fantasy
Drama
Horror
Comedy
Music
Documentary / Reality TV

In fact think of every movie genre at the Academy Awards, and there is probably a form of entertainment that you could adapt to your presentation.

Documentaries - are the stories we tell about other people. Case studies, examples, ways of getting our point across by using real-life examples.

Drama - is the archetypal before and after shots we see in weight loss advertisements, and also in rags to riches success stories. There is always a lot of drama along the way - sacrifice, emotion, hard work, lucky breaks, and more.

Action and Adventure give us a chance to live through someone elses eyes doing the things we believe we will never do ourselves. Fly a plane? Race a Formula One car? Save the world?

The movies let us do this. We can be there. We can be the one.

But for most speakers, they only seem to try and work in Comedy!

The hardest one of all.

The most important thing is to choose one, then stay focused on that niche. Don't go outside it, don't get bored with it. You need to stay in it and build and build. Then people will know the type of speaker or trainer or teacher you are. And they have confidence when you speak.

Education

We sit in front of people that we believe know more than us. Because when we sit we expect to learn. You have to provide something new for people in your audience so they can walk away thinking to themself, "Something new. Great!" At the very least something they have to think about, because if they aren't engaged and interacting, they'll be sleeping or focusing on their phone. Or the other things they could be doing right now.

In a sales presentation we present a solution to a problem. A deal. Something new.

In a motivational speech, our goal is to get an emotional reaction, a connection that creates a spark inside our audience.

When we present to the board of directors, we are showing that we have achieved things, and have a result that they can reward us for.

And if we stand in front of our children, we want them to continue believing that we know more and we know best.

We have to provide something new and interesting in our talk, or it's going to be seen and felt as a waste of time.

Value for Money

When an audience has paid for your time you have something else to consider. People have high expectations for something they paid for, and so everything they are learning, or being entertained by has a dollar value attached.

Sharing an idea for 30 minutes? That might have been $75 of their time. Did you provide at least $75 value? Or more to the point, what's their expectation of a return on investment of money. Is it 3:1, 10:1? Are you expected to create a $10,000 value for the $2000 weekend workshop they are attending?

Or have you set the expectations lower, only positioning your talk as having a potential for a 1:1 return on investment, or maybe 2:1.

My experience has been the lower the value expected, the lower the satisfaction level of the audience.

In the past they called this hype. Giving people the benefits they could experience from the talk, workshop, seminar or speech.

Now it is just a cold hard reality that if people are going to spend their money, they expect they can go back to their boss or their wife or their business partner and say how much value they can now create as a result of your talk.

I know that if I am doing a public speaking talk, I can easily show the value as being more than $100,000 - because that's the minimum I make each year as a public speaker.

I can show salesmen that the importance of understanding personalities is worth $1Million a year, because that's how I hired and trained and managed a staff of 110 people. And that was the revenue generated.

I can show you the value of getting your first impression right in online advertising, because I helped a computer software company invest less than $1000 a month in promotions for more than $15,000 a month in sales.

Value for time

The only thing equally or more valuable than money is Time.

When your audience sits down, whether its 1 or 1000, the clock starts ticking on your presentation immediately.

This is why we spend so much time in both this book and my first Volume, talking about ways to grab the audiences attention. To say the right thing. To look the right way. To engage and interact. And to create the connection you need to make your presentation successful.

Use time in 5-7 minute increments. If you have their attention now, it doesn't guarantee it continuing, but you can definitely train yourself to continue enrolling your audience throughout your talk. Through interactions both verbal and physical. Asking questions, and getting them to raise their hands and answer.

If you do that right, they not only walk out of the talk feeling like they got value, they more importantly don't feel like they wasted their time. That will get your ability as a speaker talked about and you'll get more talks.

CHAPTER THIRTEEN
Conclusion and acknowledgments

Mastery of Public Speaking

Well that's the end of the second Volume of these books.

We've discussed the amazing Power of the stage, and the keys to Mastery.

You have discovered the importance of being Local, and the interesting ways we can take in information from reading to listening to feeling and participating.

Involving your audience in your talk taught you about interaction as a tool for people getting your message more completely.

The skill of imperfection taught you why people trust some speakers and not others.

We gave you a trainers tip - how to get a standing ovation through the power of instruction.

And highlighted the use of numbers in our talk as a key focal point.

You have the power of repetition as a tool for ensuring people 'get' your message and you know how to write a talk and get your first impression right.

After more than 20 chapters across the two books and more than 44,000 words, you have an encyclopaedia of information to digest.

If you read the book from beginning to end, you might prefer to focus on just one chapter at a time when working them into your talks.

The key is to start. Volunteer to speak anywhere you can, and you'll find that people love someone who will stand up - because no-one else wants to do it!

Attend a live workshop in your area, whatever the name. Attend Toastmasters, National Speakers, your local Chamber of Commerce, or a Service group - Rotary, Lions, Apex or any other local community group that meets regularly.

If you go to MasterTheArtOfPublicSpeaking.com you'll see event schedules where I am speaking around the world, and of course you can get the free copy of my motivational quotes book, "You Don't Get Any Better At Public Speaking Sitting In Your Chair!"

Just be sure to subscribe to the list.

Next steps as always is, get up and speak somewhere!

Thanks to all the editors and reviewers, and those who wanted to be a part of this book just by being in the live events and trainings.

I wish you all the best and look forward to seeing a video, hearing an audio, or sitting in your audience one day soon.

Mark